My

GREENHOUSE

Journal

by Greta Heinen

Edited by Laurence Grigg
Cover photograph by Henry Heinen
Cover design by Jim Martin
Printed in Canada

First Printing 2003
Second Printing 2009, revised

Canadian Cataloguing in Publication Data

Heinen, Greta 1948-
My Greenhouse Journal/Greta Heinen; editor, Laurence Grigg

ISBN 0-9698030-1-X

1. Greenhouse Gardening 2. Diaries (Blank Books) I. Grigg Laurence II. Title.

SB415.H442 2003   635'.0483   C2003-910013-8

Introduction

As a greenhouse owner, you have probably read many books and articles on greenhouse gardening. The subjects range from propagating seeds and growing vegetables to the care of specialty plants such as orchids. Yet the best source of information about your greenhouse will come from the notes you record in this journal.

My Greenhouse Journal is designed for daily notes over weekly periods. It is often difficult to remember all the details about your greenhouse, and sometimes notes about your seasonal activities become misplaced. As a two-year journal, *My Greenhouse Journal* allows you to refer to last year's records so that you can plan your next greenhouse season.

Propagation records are perhaps the most important records to keep because this is the place where it all begins. When seedlings become visible, for example, you can determine when to transplant. Transplanting and flowering dates show whether the propagation dates should be earlier or later the following year. A planned schedule of fertilizing achieves the best plant results. Finally, since the chief aim of greenhouse gardening is to maintain an even or optimal environment for the plants, recording maximum and minimum temperatures will allow you to adjust the heating and cooling as required.

In the front of this book I have included an informational resource section that includes greenhouse gardening tips, greenhouse and accessory suppliers and sources of seed catalogues.

I trust that *My Greenhouse Journal* will become your most informative guide to a productive greenhouse.

	January 1		*January 2*
Temperatures:		Temperatures:	
Max:	*Min:*	*Max:*	*Min:*

	January 1		*January 2*
Temperatures:		Temperatures:	
Max:	*Min:*	*Max*	*Min:*

January 3	*January 4*
Temperatures:	Temperatures:
Max: *Min:*	*Max:* *Min:*

January 3	*January 4*
Temperatures:	Temperatures:
Max: *Min:*	*Max:* *Min:*

January 5	*January 6*
Temperatures:	Temperatures:
Max: *Min:*	*Max:* *Min:*

January 5	*January 6*
Temperatures:	Temperatures:
Max: *Min:*	*Max* *Min:*

	January 7	*Additional Greenhouse Notes:*
Temperatures:		
Max:	*Min:*	
	January 7	
Temperatures:		
Max:	*Min:*	
		Check and record maximum and minimum greenhouse temperatures daily.

	January 8		*January 9*
Temperatures:		Temperatures:	
Max:	*Min:*	*Max:*	*Min:*

	January 8		*January 9*
Temperatures:		Temperatures:	
Max:	*Min:*	*Max*	*Min:*

January 10	*January 11*
Temperatures:	Temperatures:
Max: *Min:*	*Max:* *Min:*
January 10	*January 11*
Temperatures:	Temperatures:
Max: *Min:*	*Max:* *Min:*

	January 12		*January 13*
Temperatures:		Temperatures:	
Max:	*Min:*	*Max:*	*Min:*

	January 12		*January 13*
Temperatures:		Temperatures:	
Max:	*Min:*	*Max*	*Min:*

January 14	*Additional Greenhouse Notes:*
Temperatures:	
Max: *Min:*	
January 14	
Temperatures:	
Max: *Min:*	
	Prune back vines such as the passion flower, to encourage new spring growth.

January 15	*January 16*
Temperatures:	Temperatures:
Max:　　　*Min:*	*Max:*　　　*Min:*

January 15	*January 16*
Temperatures:	Temperatures:
Max:　　　*Min:*	*Max*　　　*Min:*

January 17	*January 18*
Temperatures:	Temperatures:
Max: *Min:*	*Max:* *Min:*
January 17	*January 18*
Temperatures:	Temperatures:
Max: *Min:*	*Max:* *Min:*

	January 19		*January 20*
Temperatures:		Temperatures:	
Max: *Min:*		*Max:* *Min:*	

	January 19		*January 20*
Temperatures:		Temperatures:	
Max: *Min:*		*Max* *Min:*	

January 21	Additional Greenhouse Notes:
Temperatures:	
Max: *Min:*	
January 21	
Temperatures:	
Max: *Min:*	
	Slow growing seed varieties like the geranium are sown this month

January 22	*January 23*
Temperatures:	Temperatures:
Max: *Min:*	*Max:* *Min:*

January 22	*January 23*
Temperatures:	Temperatures:
Max: *Min:*	*Max* *Min:*

January 24	*January 25*
Temperatures:	Temperatures:
Max: *Min:*	*Max:* *Min:*

January 24	*January 25*
Temperatures:	Temperatures:
Max: *Min:*	*Max:* *Min:*

January 26	*January 27*
Temperatures:	Temperatures:
Max: *Min:*	*Max:* *Min:*

January 26	*January 27*
Temperatures:	Temperatures:
Max: *Min:*	*Max* *Min:*

January 28	*Additional Greenhouse Notes:*
Temperatures:	
Max: *Min:*	
January 28	
Temperatures:	
Max: *Min:*	
	Many plants are in the dormant stage and require very little water

	January 29		*January 30*
Temperatures:		Temperatures:	
Max: *Min:*		*Max:* *Min:*	

	January 29		*January 30*
Temperatures:		Temperatures:	
Max: *Min:*		*Max* *Min:*	

January 31	*February 1*
Temperatures:	Temperatures:
Max: *Min:*	*Max:* *Min:*

January 31	*February 1*
Temperatures:	Temperatures:
Max: *Min:*	*Max:* *Min:*

	February 2		*February 3*
Temperatures:		Temperatures:	
Max:	*Min:*	*Max:*	*Min:*

	February 2		*February 3*
Temperatures:		Temperatures:	
Max:	*Min:*	*Max*	*Min:*

	February 4	Additional Greenhouse Notes:
Temperatures:		
Max: Min:		
	February 4	
Temperatures:		
Max: Min:		
		A small circulating fan can help to control condensation.

	February 5		*February 6*
Temperatures:		Temperatures:	
Max: *Min:*		*Max:* *Min:*	
	February 5		*February 6*
Temperatures:		Temperatures:	
Max: *Min:*		*Max* *Min:*	

February 7	*February 8*
Temperatures:	Temperatures:
Max: *Min:*	*Max:* *Min:*

February 7	*February 8*
Temperatures:	Temperatures:
Max: *Min:*	*Max:* *Min:*

February 9	*February 10*
Temperatures:	Temperatures:
Max: *Min:*	*Max:* *Min:*

February 9	*February 10*
Temperatures:	Temperatures:
Max: *Min:*	*Max* *Min:*

	February 11	*Additional Greenhouse Notes:*
Temperatures:		
Max:	*Min:*	

	February 11	
Temperatures:		
Max:	*Min:*	
		Start early vegetable crop in the greenhouse this month.

February 12	*February 13*
Temperatures:	Temperatures:
Max: *Min:*	*Max:* *Min:*

February 12	*February 13*
Temperatures:	Temperatures:
Max: *Min:*	*Max* *Min:*

February 14	*February 15*
Temperatures:	Temperatures:
Max: *Min:*	*Max:* *Min:*
February 14	*February 15*
Temperatures:	Temperatures:
Max: *Min:*	*Max:* *Min:*

	February 16		February 17
Temperatures:		Temperatures:	
Max:	*Min:*	*Max:*	*Min:*

	February 16		February 17
Temperatures:		Temperatures:	
Max:	*Min:*	*Max*	*Min:*

	February 18	*Additional Greenhouse Notes:*
Temperatures:		
Max:	*Min:*	
	February 18	
Temperatures:		
Max:	*Min:*	
		Start tuberous begonias in small pots and placed on a heated propagating bed.

February 19	*February 20*
Temperatures:	Temperatures:
Max: *Min:*	*Max:* *Min:*

February 19	*February 20*
Temperatures:	Temperatures:
Max: *Min:*	*Max* *Min:*

February 21	*February 22*
Temperatures:	Temperatures:
Max: *Min:*	*Max:* *Min:*

February 21	*February 22*
Temperatures:	Temperatures:
Max: *Min:*	*Max:* *Min*

	February 23		February 24
Temperatures:		Temperatures:	
Max:	Min:	Max:	Min:

	February 23		February 24
Temperatures:		Temperatures:	
Max:	Min:	Max	Min:

	February 25	_Additional Greenhouse Notes:_
Temperatures:		
Max:	_Min:_	
	February 25	
Temperatures:		
Max:	_Min:_	
		Check plants regularly for early detection of pests or diseases.

February 26	*February 27*
Temperatures:	Temperatures:
Max: *Min:*	*Max:* *Min:*

February 26	*February 27*
Temperatures:	Temperatures:
Max: *Min:*	*Max* *Min:*

36

	February 28		*March 1*
Temperatures:		Temperatures:	
Max:	*Min:*	*Max:*	*Min:*
	February 28		*March 1*
Temperatures:		Temperatures:	
Max:	*Min:*	*Max:*	*Min:*

	March 2		*March 3*
Temperatures:		Temperatures:	
Max:	*Min:*	*Max:*	*Min:*

	March 2		*March 3*
Temperatures:		Temperatures:	
Max:	*Min:*	*Max*	*Min:*

	March 4	*Additional Greenhouse Notes:*
Temperatures:		
Max:	*Min:*	
	March 4	
Temperatures:		
Max:	*Min:*	
		Sow annual bedding plant seeds, which need bottom heat to germinate.

March 5	*March 6*
Temperatures:	Temperatures:
Max: *Min:*	*Max:* *Min:*

March 5	*March 6*
Temperatures:	Temperatures:
Max: *Min:*	*Max* *Min:*

	March 7		*March 8*
Temperatures:		Temperatures:	
Max:	*Min:*	*Max:*	*Min:*

	March 7		*March 8*
Temperatures:		Temperatures:	
Max:	*Min:*	*Max:*	*Min:*

	March 9		*March 10*
Temperatures:		Temperatures:	
Max:	*Min:*	*Max:*	*Min:*
	March 9		*March 10*
Temperatures:		Temperatures:	
Max:	*Min:*	*Max*	*Min:*

March 11	Additional Greenhouse Notes:
Temperatures:	
Max: Min:	
March 11	
Temperatures:	
Max: Min:	
	Use a grow light for additional hours of light give a boost to cuttings and seedlings.

March 12	*March 13*
Temperatures:	Temperatures:
Max: *Min:*	*Max:* *Min:*

March 12	*March 13*
Temperatures:	Temperatures:
Max: *Min:*	*Max* *Min:*

March 14	March 15
Temperatures:	Temperatures:
Max: *Min:*	*Max:* *Min:*

March 14	March 15
Temperatures:	Temperatures:
Max: *Min:*	*Max:* *Min:*

	March 16		*March 17*
Temperatures:		Temperatures:	
Max: *Min:*		*Max:* *Min:*	

	March 16		*March 17*
Temperatures:		Temperatures:	
Max: *Min:*		*Max* *Min:*	

	March 18	Additional Greenhouse Notes:
Temperatures:		
Max:	Min:	
	March 18	
Temperatures:		
Max:	Min:	
		An exterior shade cloth will prevent heat build up inside the greenhouse.

March 19	March 20
Temperatures:	Temperatures:
Max: Min:	Max: Min:

March 19	March 20
Temperatures:	Temperatures:
Max: Min:	Max Min:

	March 21		*March 22*
Temperatures:		Temperatures:	
Max: *Min:*		*Max:* *Min:*	

	March 21		*March 22*
Temperatures:		Temperatures:	
Max: *Min:*		*Max:* *Min:*	

	March 23		*March 24*
Temperatures:		Temperatures:	
Max:	*Min:*	*Max:*	*Min:*

	March 23		*March 24*
Temperatures:		Temperatures:	
Max:	*Min:*	*Max*	*Min:*

	March 25	*Additional Greenhouse Notes:*
Temperatures:		
Max:	*Min:*	
	March 25	
Temperatures:		
Max:	*Min:*	
		Keep seedlings moist and provide shading to protect the seedlings from the sun's burning rays.

March 26	*March 27*
Temperatures:	Temperatures:
Max: *Min:*	*Max:* *Min:*

March 26	*March 27*
Temperatures:	Temperatures:
Max: *Min:*	*Max* *Min:*

March 28	March 29
Temperatures:	Temperatures:
Max: Min:	Max: Min:

March 28	March 29
Temperatures:	Temperatures:
Max: Min:	Max: Min:

March 30		*March 31*	
Temperatures:		Temperatures:	
Max:	*Min:*	*Max:*	*Min:*
March 30		*March 31*	
Temperatures:		Temperatures:	
Max:	*Min:*	*Max*	*Min:*

	April 1	Additional Greenhouse Notes:
Temperatures:		
Max:	Min:	
	April 1	
Temperatures:		
Max:	Min:	
		Sow cucumber and tomato seeds for a summer crop in the greenhouse.

	April 2		*April 3*
Temperatures:		Temperatures:	
Max: *Min:*		*Max:* *Min:*	

	April 2		*April 3*
Temperatures:		Temperatures:	
Max: *Min:*		*Max* *Min:*	

	April 4		*April 5*
Temperatures:		Temperatures:	
Max:	*Min:*	*Max:*	*Min:*

	April 4		*April 5*
Temperatures:		Temperatures:	
Max:	*Min:*	*Max:*	*Min:*

	April 6		*April 7*
Temperatures:		Temperatures:	
Max:	*Min:*	*Max:*	*Min:*

	April 6		*April 7*
Temperatures:		Temperatures:	
Max:	*Min:*	*Max*	*Min:*

	April 8	Additional Greenhouse Notes:
Temperatures:		
Max:	Min:	
	April 8	
Temperatures:		
Max:	Min:	
		Since spring temperatures fluctuate, check the greenhouse thermometer to make sure the greenhouse has adequate ventilation.

	April 9		*April 10*
Temperatures:		Temperatures:	
Max:	*Min:*	*Max:*	*Min:*

	April 9		*April 10*
Temperatures:		Temperatures:	
Max:	*Min:*	*Max*	*Min:*

April 11	*April 12*
Temperatures:	Temperatures:
Max: *Min:*	*Max:* *Min:*

April 11	*April 12*
Temperatures:	Temperatures:
Max: *Min:*	*Max:* *Min:*

	April 13		April 14
Temperatures:		Temperatures:	
Max:	*Min:*	*Max:*	*Min:*

	April 13		April 14
Temperatures:		Temperatures:	
Max:	*Min:*	*Max*	*Min:*

	April 15	*Additional Greenhouse Notes:*
Temperatures:		
Max:	*Min:*	
	April 15	
Temperatures:		
Max:	*Min:*	
		Transplant seedlings and start a fertilizing schedule.

	April 16		*April 17*
Temperatures:		Temperatures:	
Max:	*Min:*	*Max:*	*Min:*

	April 16		*April 17*
Temperatures:		Temperatures:	
Max:	*Min:*	*Max*	*Min:*

	April 18		April 19
Temperatures:		Temperatures:	
Max:	*Min:*	*Max:*	*Min:*

	April 18		April 19
Temperatures:		Temperatures:	
Max:	*Min:*	*Max:*	*Min:*

	April 20		*April 21*
Temperatures:		Temperatures:	
Max:	*Min:*	*Max:*	*Min:*

	April 20		*April 21*
Temperatures:		Temperatures:	
Max:	*Min:*	*Max*	*Min:*

	April 22	*Additional Greenhouse Notes:*
Temperatures:		
Max:	*Min:*	
	April 22	
Temperatures:		
Max:	*Min:*	
		Prepare and make hanging baskets from cuttings and annual bedding plants.

	April 23		*April 24*
Temperatures:		Temperatures:	
Max: *Min:*		*Max:* *Min:*	

	April 23		*April 24*
Temperatures:		Temperatures:	
Max: *Min:*		*Max* *Min:*	

	April 25		*April 26*
Temperatures:		Temperatures:	
Max: *Min:*		*Max:* *Min:*	

	April 25		*April 26*
Temperatures:		Temperatures:	
Max: *Min:*		*Max:* *Min:*	

	April 27		April 28
Temperatures:		Temperatures:	
Max:	Min:	Max:	Min:

	April 27		April 28
Temperatures:		Temperatures:	
Max:	Min:	Max	Min:

	April 29	Additional Greenhouse Notes:
Temperatures:		
Max:	Min:	
	April 29	
Temperatures:		
Max:	Min:	
		Pinch back seedlings and cuttings to encourage new branches.

	April 30		*May 1*
Temperatures:		Temperatures:	
Max: *Min:*		*Max:* *Min:*	

	April 30		*May 1*
Temperatures:		Temperatures:	
Max: *Min:*		*Max* *Min:*	

	May 2		May 3
Temperatures:		Temperatures:	
Max:	Min:	Max:	Min:

	May 2		May 3
Temperatures:		Temperatures:	
Max:	Min:	Max:	Min:

	May 4		*May 5*
Temperatures:		Temperatures:	
Max:	*Min:*	*Max:*	*Min:*

	May 4		*May 5*
Temperatures:		Temperatures:	
Max:	*Min:*	*Max*	*Min:*

	May 6	_Additional Greenhouse Notes:_
Temperatures:		
Max: _Min:_		
	May 6	
Temperatures:		
Max: _Min:_		
		Plan and circle the dates for fertilizing all garden and greenhouse plants.

	May 7		*May 8*
Temperatures:		Temperatures:	
Max:	*Min:*	*Max:*	*Min:*

	May 7		*May 8*
Temperatures:		Temperatures:	
Max:	*Min:*	*Max*	*Min:*

	May 9		*May 10*
Temperatures:		Temperatures:	
Max:	*Min:*	*Max:*	*Min:*
	May 9		*May 10*
Temperatures:		Temperatures:	
Max:	*Min:*	*Max:*	*Min:*

	May 11		*May 12*
Temperatures:		Temperatures:	
Max:	*Min:*	*Max:*	*Min:*

	May 11		*May 12*
Temperatures:		Temperatures:	
Max:	*Min:*	*Max*	*Min:*

	May 13	*Additional Greenhouse Notes:*
Temperatures:		
Max:	*Min:*	
	May 13	
Temperatures:		
Max:	*Min:*	
		Move bedding plants to a protected area outside so that they can acclimatize.

May 14	*May 15*
Temperatures:	Temperatures:
Max: *Min:*	*Max:* *Min:*

May 14	*May 15*
Temperatures:	Temperatures:
Max: *Min:*	*Max* *Min:*

May 16	_May 17_
Temperatures:	Temperatures:
Max: _Min:_	_Max:_ _Min:_

May 16	_May 17_
Temperatures:	Temperatures:
Max: _Min:_	_Max:_ _Min:_

	May 18		*May 19*
Temperatures:		Temperatures:	
Max:	*Min:*	*Max:*	*Min:*

	May 18		*May 19*
Temperatures:		Temperatures:	
Max:	*Min:*	*Max*	*Min:*

	May 20	Additional Greenhouse Notes:
Temperatures:		
Max:	Min:	
	May 20	
Temperatures:		
Max:	Min:	
		Transplant the greenhouse cucumbers and tomatoes to a soil bed or container.

May 21	*May 22*
Temperatures:	Temperatures:
Max: *Min:*	*Max:* *Min:*

May 21	*May 22*
Temperatures:	Temperatures:
Max: *Min:*	*Max* *Min:*

	May 23		*May 24*
Temperatures:		Temperatures:	
Max: *Min:*		*Max:* *Min:*	

	May 23		*May 24*
Temperatures:		Temperatures:	
Max: *Min:*		*Max:* *Min:*	

	May 25		*May 26*
Temperatures:		Temperatures:	
Max:	*Min:*	*Max:*	*Min:*

	May 25		*May 26*
Temperatures:		Temperatures:	
Max:	*Min:*	*Max*	*Min:*

	May 27	*Additional Greenhouse Notes:*
Temperatures:		
Max: *Min:*		
	May 27	
Temperatures:		
Max: *Min:*		
		You must water greenhouse plants regularly and maintain greenhouse humidity.

	May 28		*May 29*
Temperatures:		Temperatures:	
Max:	*Min:*	*Max:*	*Min:*

	May 28		*May 29*
Temperatures:		Temperatures:	
Max:	*Min:*	*Max*	*Min:*

	May 30		*May 31*
Temperatures:		Temperatures:	
Max:	*Min:*	*Max:*	*Min:*
	May 30		*May 31*
Temperatures:		Temperatures:	
Max:	*Min:*	*Max:*	*Min:*

	June 1		*June 2*
Temperatures:		Temperatures:	
Max:	*Min:*	*Max:*	*Min:*

	June 1		*June 2*
Temperatures:		Temperatures:	
Max:	*Min:*	*Max*	*Min:*

	June 3	*Additional Greenhouse Notes:*
Temperatures:		
Max:	*Min:*	
	June 3	
Temperatures:		
Max:	*Min:*	
		Clean and store heating equipment and insulating materials

	June 4		*June 5*
Temperatures:		Temperatures:	
Max:	*Min:*	*Max:*	*Min:*

	June 4		*June 5*
Temperatures:		Temperatures:	
Max:	*Min:*	*Max*	*Min:*

	June 6		*June 7*
Temperatures:		Temperatures:	
Max:	*Min:*	*Max:*	*Min:*

	June 6		*June 7*
Temperatures:		Temperatures:	
Max:	*Min:*	*Max:*	*Min:*

June 8	*June 9*
Temperatures:	Temperatures:
Max: *Min:*	*Max:* *Min:*

June 8	*June 9*
Temperatures:	Temperatures:
Max: *Min:*	*Max* *Min:*

	June 10	Additional Greenhouse Notes:
Temperatures:		
Max:	Min:	
	June 10	
Temperatures:		
Max:	Min:	
		Stake the greenhouse cucumber and tomato plants.

	June 11		*June 12*
Temperatures:		Temperatures:	
Max:	*Min:*	*Max:*	*Min:*

	June 11		*June 12*
Temperatures:		Temperatures:	
Max:	*Min:*	*Max*	*Min:*

June 13	*June 14*
Temperatures:	Temperatures:
Max: *Min:*	*Max:* *Min:*

June 13	*June 14*
Temperatures:	Temperatures:
Max: *Min:*	*Max:* *Min:*

June 15	*June 16*
Temperatures:	Temperatures:
Max: *Min:*	*Max:* *Min:*

June 15	*June 16*
Temperatures:	Temperatures:
Max: *Min:*	*Max* *Min:*

June 17	Additional Greenhouse Notes:
Temperatures:	
Max: Min:	
June 17	
Temperatures:	
Max: Min:	
	Tap the staked cucumber and tomato plants daily to ensure pollination.

	June 18		*June 19*
Temperatures:		Temperatures:	
Max:	*Min:*	*Max:*	*Min:*

	June 18		*June 19*
Temperatures:		Temperatures:	
Max:	*Min:*	*Max*	*Min:*

	June 20		*June 21*
Temperatures:		Temperatures:	
Max:	*Min:*	*Max:*	*Min:*

	June 20		*June 21*
Temperatures:		Temperatures:	
Max:	*Min:*	*Max:*	*Min:*

June 22	*June 23*
Temperatures:	Temperatures:
Max: *Min:*	*Max:* *Min:*

June 22	*June 23*
Temperatures:	Temperatures:
Max: *Min:*	*Max* *Min:*

June 24	*Additional Greenhouse Notes:*
Temperatures:	
Max: *Min:*	
June 24	
Temperatures:	
Max: *Min:*	
	Automatic vent openers assist in controlling the greenhouse temperature.

June 25	*June 26*
Temperatures:	Temperatures:
Max: *Min:*	*Max:* *Min:*

June 25	*June 26*
Temperatures:	Temperatures:
Max: *Min:*	*Max* *Min:*

	June 27		*June 28*
Temperatures:		Temperatures:	
Max:	*Min:*	*Max:*	*Min:*

	June 27		*June 28*
Temperatures:		Temperatures:	
Max:	*Min:*	*Max:*	*Min:*

June 29	*June 30*
Temperatures:	Temperatures:
Max: *Min:*	*Max:* *Min:*

June 29	*June 30*
Temperatures:	Temperatures:
Max: *Min:*	*Max* *Min:*

	July 1	Additional Greenhouse Notes:
Temperatures:		
Max:	Min:	
	July 1	
Temperatures:		
Max:	Min:	
		Damp down the greenhouse to cool the atmosphere on hot days.

	July 2		*July 3*
Temperatures:		Temperatures:	
Max:	*Min:*	*Max:*	*Min:*

	July 2		*July 3*
Temperatures:		Temperatures:	
Max:	*Min:*	*Max*	*Min:*

	July 4		*July 5*
Temperatures:		Temperatures:	
Max:	*Min:*	*Max:*	*Min:*

	July 4		*July 5*
Temperatures:		Temperatures:	
Max:	*Min:*	*Max:*	*Min:*

	July 6		*July 7*
Temperatures:		Temperatures:	
Max:	*Min:*	*Max:*	*Min:*

	July 6		*July 7*
Temperatures:		Temperatures:	
Max:	*Min:*	*Max*	*Min:*

	July 8	Additional Greenhouse Notes:
Temperatures:		
Max:　　　　Min:		
	July 8	
Temperatures:		
Max:　　　　Min:		
		Watch for pests and diseases during the hot summer months.

July 9	July 10
Temperatures:	Temperatures:
Max: Min:	Max: Min:

July 9	July 10
Temperatures:	Temperatures:
Max: Min:	Max Min:

July 11	*July 12*
Temperatures:	Temperatures:
Max: *Min:*	*Max:* *Min:*

July 11	*July 12*
Temperatures:	Temperatures:
Max: *Min:*	*Max:* *Min:*

	July 13		July 14
Temperatures:		Temperatures:	
Max:	Min:	Max:	Min:

	July 13		July 14
Temperatures:		Temperatures:	
Max:	Min:	Max	Min:

	July 15	*Additional Greenhouse Notes:*
Temperatures:		
Max:	*Min:*	
	July 15	
Temperatures:		
Max:	*Min:*	
		Regularly feed the cucumbers and tomatoes. Pinch back the "suckers" on tomato plants.

	July 16		*July 17*
Temperatures:		Temperatures:	
Max: *Min:*		*Max:* *Min:*	

	July 16		*July 17*
Temperatures:		Temperatures:	
Max: *Min:*		*Max* *Min:*	

July 18	*July 19*
Temperatures:	Temperatures:
Max: *Min:*	*Max:* *Min:*

July 18	*July 19*
Temperatures:	Temperatures:
Max: *Min:*	*Max:* *Min:*

	July 20		*July 21*
Temperatures:		Temperatures:	
Max:	*Min:*	*Max:*	*Min:*

	July 20		*July 21*
Temperatures:		Temperatures:	
Max:	*Min:*	*Max*	*Min:*

	July 22	Additional Greenhouse Notes:
Temperatures:		
Max:	Min:	
	July 22	
Temperatures:		
Max:	Min:	
		Increase water to allow greenhouse cacti to bloom.

July 23	*July 24*
Temperatures:	Temperatures:
Max: *Min:*	*Max:* *Min:*
July 23	*July 24*
Temperatures:	Temperatures:
Max: *Min:*	*Max* *Min:*

	July 25		*July 26*
Temperatures:		Temperatures:	
Max:	*Min:*	*Max:*	*Min:*

	July 25		*July 26*
Temperatures:		Temperatures:	
Max:	*Min:*	*Max:*	*Min:*

	July 27		*July 28*
Temperatures:		Temperatures:	
Max:	*Min:*	*Max:*	*Min:*

	July 27		*July 28*
Temperatures:		Temperatures:	
Max:	*Min:*	*Max:*	*Min:*

	July 29	*Additional Greenhouse Notes:*

Temperatures:

Max: *Min:*

	July 29	

Temperatures:

Max: *Min:*

Check greenhouse temperatures.
An exhaust fan may be required.

July 30	*July 31*
Temperatures:	Temperatures:
Max: *Min:*	*Max:* *Min:*

July 30	*July 31*
Temperatures:	Temperatures:
Max: *Min:*	*Max* *Min:*

	August 1		*August 2*
Temperatures:		Temperatures:	
Max: *Min:*		*Max:* *Min:*	
	August 1		*August 2*
Temperatures:		Temperatures:	
Max: *Min:*		*Max:* *Min:*	

	August 3		August 4
Temperatures:		Temperatures:	
Max:	*Min:*	*Max:*	*Min:*

	August 3		August 4
Temperatures:		Temperatures:	
Max:	*Min:*	*Max*	*Min:*

	August 5	Additional Greenhouse Notes:
Temperatures:		
Max:	*Min:*	

	August 5	
Temperatures:		
Max:	*Min:*	
		Take cuttings from the garden plants.

August 6	*August 7*
Temperatures:	Temperatures:
Max: *Min:*	*Max:* *Min:*

August 6	*August 7*
Temperatures:	Temperatures:
Max: *Min:*	*Max* *Min:*

	August 8		*August 9*
Temperatures:		Temperatures:	
Max:	*Min:*	*Max:*	*Min:*

	August 8		*August 9*
Temperatures:		Temperatures:	
Max:	*Min:*	*Max:*	*Min:*

August 10	*August 11*
Temperatures:	Temperatures:
Max: *Min:*	*Max:* *Min:*

August 10	*August 11*
Temperatures:	Temperatures:
Max: *Min:*	*Max* *Min:*

	August 12	_Additional Greenhouse Notes:_
Temperatures:		
Max:	_Min:_	
	August 12	
Temperatures:		
Max:	_Min:_	
		House plants will enjoy the humidity of the greenhouse.

August 13	*August 14*
Temperatures:	Temperatures:
Max: *Min:*	*Max:* *Min:*

August 13	*August 14*
Temperatures:	Temperatures:
Max: *Min:*	*Max* *Min:*

	August 15		*August 16*
Temperatures:		Temperatures:	
Max:	*Min:*	*Max:*	*Min:*

	August 15		*August 16*
Temperatures:		Temperatures:	
Max:	*Min:*	*Max:*	*Min:*

	August 17		*August 18*
Temperatures:		Temperatures:	
Max:	*Min:*	*Max:*	*Min:*

	August 17		*August 18*
Temperatures:		Temperatures:	
Max:	*Min:*	*Max*	*Min:*

	August 19	*Additional Greenhouse Notes:*
Temperatures:		
Max: *Min:*		
	August 19	
Temperatures:		
Max: *Min:*		
		Dead-head greenhouse plants to extend the flowering season.

	August 20		*August 21*
Temperatures:		Temperatures:	
Max:	*Min:*	*Max:*	*Min:*

	August 20		*August 21*
Temperatures:		Temperatures:	
Max:	*Min:*	*Max*	*Min:*

August 22	*August 23*
Temperatures:	Temperatures:
Max: *Min:*	*Max:* *Min:*

August 22	*August 23*
Temperatures:	Temperatures:
Max: *Min:*	*Max:* *Min:*

	August 24		*August 25*
Temperatures:		Temperatures:	
Max: *Min:*		*Max:* *Min:*	
	August 24		*August 25*
Temperatures:		Temperatures:	
Max: *Min:*		*Max* *Min:*	

	August 26	*Additional Greenhouse Notes:*
Temperatures:		
Max:	*Min:*	
	August 26	
Temperatures:		
Max:	*Min:*	
		Discard old leaves and fallen fruit around the cucumber and tomatoes to prevent disease.

August 27	*August 28*
Temperatures:	Temperatures:
Max: *Min:*	*Max:* *Min:*

August 27	*August 28*
Temperatures:	Temperatures:
Max: *Min:*	*Max* *Min:*

August 29	*August 30*
Temperatures:	Temperatures:
Max:　　　　*Min:*	*Max:*　　　　*Min:*

August 29	*August 30*
Temperatures:	Temperatures:
Max:　　　　*Min:*	*Max:*　　　　*Min:*

	August 31		*September 1*
Temperatures:		Temperatures:	
Max:	*Min:*	*Max:*	*Min:*
	August 31		*September 1*
Temperatures:		Temperatures:	
Max:	*Min:*	*Max*	*Min:*

	September 2	*Additional Greenhouse Notes:*
Temperatures:		
Max: *Min:*		
	September 2	
Temperatures:		
Max: *Min:*		
		Check heating systems since an early frost is possible in the cooler climates.

143

September 3	*September 4*
Temperatures:	Temperatures:
Max: *Min:*	*Max:* *Min:*

September 3	*September 4*
Temperatures:	Temperatures:
Max: *Min:*	*Max* *Min:*

	September 5		*September 6*
Temperatures:		Temperatures:	
Max:	*Min:*	*Max:*	*Min:*

	September 5		*September 6*
Temperatures:		Temperatures:	
Max:	*Min:*	*Max:*	*Min:*

September 7	*September 8*
Temperatures:	Temperatures:
Max: *Min:*	*Max:* *Min:*

September 7	*September 8*
Temperatures:	Temperatures:
Max: *Min:*	*Max* *Min:*

September 9	Additional Greenhouse Notes:
Temperatures:	
Max: Min:	
September 9	
Temperatures:	
Max: Min:	
	Remove shading material and give the greenhouse its annual cleaning.

	September 10		September 11
Temperatures:		Temperatures:	
Max:	Min:	Max:	Min:

	September 10		September 11
Temperatures:		Temperatures:	
Max:	Min:	Max	Min:

	September 12		September 13
Temperatures:		Temperatures:	
Max:	Min:	Max:	Min:

	September 12		September 13
Temperatures:		Temperatures:	
Max:	Min:	Max:	Min:

	September 14		*September 15*
Temperatures:		Temperatures:	
Max:	*Min:*	*Max:*	*Min:*

	September 14		*September 15*
Temperatures:		Temperatures:	
Max:	*Min:*	*Max*	*Min:*

September 16	Additional Greenhouse Notes:
Temperatures:	
Max: Min:	
September 16	
Temperatures:	
Max: Min:	
	Cut back the frost-sensitive plants. They will over winter in the greenhouse.

September 17	*September 18*
Temperatures:	Temperatures:
Max: *Min:*	*Max:* *Min:*

September 17	*September 18*
Temperatures:	Temperatures:
Max: *Min:*	*Max* *Min:*

September 19	*September 20*
Temperatures:	Temperatures:
Max: *Min:*	*Max:* *Min:*

September 19	*September 20*
Temperatures:	Temperatures:
Max: *Min:*	*Max:* *Min:*

September 21	September 22
Temperatures:	Temperatures:
Max: *Min:*	*Max:* *Min:*

September 21	September 22
Temperatures:	Temperatures:
Max: *Min:*	*Max* *Min:*

	September 23	*Additional Greenhouse Notes:*
Temperatures:		
Max:	*Min:*	
	September 23	
Temperatures:		
Max:	*Min:*	
		Transplant last months cuttings into 4" pots.

	September 24		*September 25*
Temperatures:		Temperatures:	
Max: *Min:*		*Max:* *Min:*	

	September 24		*September 25*
Temperatures:		Temperatures:	
Max: *Min:*		*Max* *Min:*	

	September 26		September 27
Temperatures:		Temperatures:	
Max:	Min:	Max:	Min:

	September 26		September 27
Temperatures:		Temperatures:	
Max:	Min:	Max:	Min:

	September 28		September 29
Temperatures:		Temperatures:	
Max:	Min:	Max:	Min:

	September 28		September 29
Temperatures:		Temperatures:	
Max:	Min:	Max	Min:

September 30	Additional Greenhouse Notes:
Temperatures:	
Max: Min:	
September 30	
Temperatures:	
Max: Min:	
	Clean plants with insecticide soap when bringing them into the greenhouse as a preventative measure.

	October 1		*October 2*
Temperatures:		Temperatures:	
Max: *Min:*		*Max:* *Min:*	

	October 1		*October 2*
Temperatures:		Temperatures:	
Max: *Min:*		*Max* *Min:*	

	October 3		*October 4*
Temperatures:		Temperatures:	
Max:	*Min:*	*Max:*	*Min:*

	October 3		*October 4*
Temperatures:		Temperatures:	
Max:	*Min:*	*Max:*	*Min:*

October 5	*October 6*
Temperatures:	Temperatures:
Max:　　　　*Min:*	*Max:*　　　　*Min:*

October 5	*October 6*
Temperatures:	Temperatures:
Max:　　　　*Min:*	*Max*　　　　*Min:*

	October 7	Additional Greenhouse Notes:
Temperatures:		
Max:	Min:	
	October 7	
Temperatures:		
Max:	Min:	
		Plant bulbs in containers for winter blooms. Place them in a dark cool place.

October 8	*October 9*
Temperatures:	Temperatures:
Max: *Min:*	*Max:* *Min:*

October 8	*October 9*
Temperatures:	Temperatures:
Max: *Min:*	*Max* *Min:*

October 10	*October 11*
Temperatures:	Temperatures:
Max: *Min:*	*Max:* *Min:*
October 10	*October 11*
Temperatures:	Temperatures:
Max: *Min:*	*Max:* *Min:*

October 12	*October 13*
Temperatures:	Temperatures:
Max: *Min:*	*Max:* *Min:*

October 12	*October 13*
Temperatures:	Temperatures:
Max: *Min:*	*Max* *Min:*

	October 14	*Additional Greenhouse Notes:*
Temperatures:		
Max:	*Min:*	
	October 14	
Temperatures:		
Max:	*Min:*	
		Bring in frost-sensitive plants in warmer climates.

	October 15		*October 16*
Temperatures:		Temperatures:	
Max: *Min:*		*Max:* *Min:*	

	October 15		*October 16*
Temperatures:		Temperatures:	
Max: *Min:*		*Max* *Min:*	

	October 17		*October 18*
Temperatures:		Temperatures:	
Max:	*Min:*	*Max:*	*Min:*

	October 17		*October 18*
Temperatures:		Temperatures:	
Max:	*Min:*	*Max:*	*Min:*

	October 19		*October 20*
Temperatures:		Temperatures:	
Max:	*Min:*	*Max:*	*Min:*

	October 19		*October 20*
Temperatures:		Temperatures:	
Max:	*Min:*	*Max*	*Min:*

	October 21	Additional Greenhouse Notes:
Temperatures:		
Max:	Min:	
	October 21	
Temperatures:		
Max:	Min:	
		Decrease watering since many plants are dormant (although they are developing root growth).

October 22	*October 23*
Temperatures:	Temperatures:
Max:　　　*Min:*	*Max:*　　　*Min:*

October 22	*October 23*
Temperatures:	Temperatures:
Max:　　　*Min:*	*Max*　　　*Min:*

	October 24		*October 25*
Temperatures:		Temperatures:	
Max:	*Min:*	*Max:*	*Min:*

	October 24		*October 25*
Temperatures:		Temperatures:	
Max:	*Min:*	*Max:*	*Min:*

	October 26		October 27
Temperatures:		Temperatures:	
Max:	*Min:*	*Max:*	*Min:*

	October 26		October 27
Temperatures:		Temperatures:	
Max:	*Min:*	*Max*	*Min:*

	October 28	*Additional Greenhouse Notes:*
Temperatures:		
Max:	*Min:*	
	October 28	
Temperatures:		
Max:	*Min:*	
		Allow some ventilation on warm fall days.

	October 29		*October 30*
Temperatures:		Temperatures:	
Max:	*Min:*	*Max:*	*Min:*

	October 29		*October 30*
Temperatures:		Temperatures:	
Max:	*Min:*	*Max*	*Min:*

	October 31		*November 1*
Temperatures:		Temperatures:	
Max:	*Min:*	*Max:*	*Min:*

	October 31		*November 1*
Temperatures:		Temperatures:	
Max:	*Min:*	*Max:*	*Min:*

November 2	*November 3*
Temperatures:	Temperatures:
Max: *Min:*	*Max:* *Min:*

November 2	*November 3*
Temperatures:	Temperatures:
Max: *Min:*	*Max* *Min:*

November 4	*Additional Greenhouse Notes:*
Temperatures:	
Max: *Min:*	
November 4	
Temperatures:	
Max: *Min:*	
	Give a little water to the Christmas cactus so that the flower buds will form.

	November 5		*November 6*
Temperatures:		Temperatures:	
Max:	*Min:*	*Max:*	*Min:*

	November 5		*November 6*
Temperatures:		Temperatures:	
Max:	*Min:*	*Max*	*Min:*

November 7	*November 8*
Temperatures:	Temperatures:
Max: *Min:*	*Max:* *Min:*

November 7	*November 8*
Temperatures:	Temperatures:
Max: *Min:*	*Max:* *Min:*

	November 9		November 10
Temperatures:		Temperatures:	
Max:	Min:	Max:	Min:

	November 9		November 10
Temperatures:		Temperatures:	
Max:	Min:	Max	Min:

	Additional Greenhouse Notes:
November 11	
Temperatures:	
Max: *Min:*	
November 11	
Temperatures:	
Max: *Min:*	
	Give a little water to the bulb containers.

	November 12		*November 13*
Temperatures:		Temperatures:	
Max:	*Min:*	*Max:*	*Min:*

	November 12		*November 13*
Temperatures:		Temperatures:	
Max:	*Min:*	*Max*	*Min:*

	November 14		*November 15*
Temperatures:		Temperatures:	
Max: *Min:*		*Max:* *Min:*	

	November 14		*November 15*
Temperatures:		Temperatures:	
Max: *Min:*		*Max:* *Min:*	

November 16	November 17
Temperatures:	Temperatures:
Max: *Min:*	*Max:* *Min:*

November 16	November 17
Temperatures:	Temperatures:
Max: *Min:*	*Max* *Min:*

November 18	*Additional Greenhouse Notes:*
Temperatures:	
Max: *Min:*	
November 18	
Temperatures:	
Max: *Min:*	
	A small circulating fan will create air movement in the greenhouse.

	November 19		*November 20*
Temperatures:		Temperatures:	
Max: *Min:*		*Max:* *Min:*	

	November 19		*November 20*
Temperatures:		Temperatures:	
Max: *Min:*		*Max* *Min:*	

November 21	*November 22*
Temperatures:	Temperatures:
Max: *Min:*	*Max:* *Min:*

November 21	*November 22*
Temperatures:	Temperatures:
Max: *Min:*	*Max:* *Min:*

	November 23		*November 24*
Temperatures:		Temperatures:	
Max:	*Min:*	*Max:*	*Min:*

	November 23		*November 24*
Temperatures:		Temperatures:	
Max:	*Min:*	*Max*	*Min:*

	November 25	*Additional Greenhouse Notes:*
Temperatures:		
Max:	*Min:*	
	November 25	
Temperatures:		
Max:	*Min:*	
		Inspect plants and remove yellowing leaves. Isolate any problem plants.

November 26	*November 27*
Temperatures:	Temperatures:
Max: *Min:*	*Max:* *Min:*

November 26	*November 27*
Temperatures:	Temperatures:
Max: *Min:*	*Max* *Min:*

November 28	*November 29*
Temperatures:	Temperatures:
Max: *Min:*	*Max:* *Min:*

November 28	*November 29*
Temperatures:	Temperatures:
Max: *Min:*	*Max:* *Min:*

November 30	*December 1*
Temperatures:	Temperatures:
Max: *Min:*	*Max:* *Min:*

November 30	*December 1*
Temperatures:	Temperatures:
Max: *Min:*	*Max* *Min:*

	December 2	Additional Greenhouse Notes:
Temperatures:		
Max:	Min:	
	December 2	
Temperatures:		
Max:	Min:	
		Place the Christmas cactus in the warmst and brightest location in the greenhouse.

December 3	December 4
Temperatures:	Temperatures:
Max: *Min:*	*Max:* *Min:*
December 3	December 4
Temperatures:	Temperatures:
Max: *Min:*	*Max* *Min:*

	December 5		*December 6*
Temperatures:		Temperatures:	
Max:	*Min:*	*Max:*	*Min:*

	December 5		*December 6*
Temperatures:		Temperatures:	
Max:	*Min:*	*Max:*	*Min:*

	December 7		*December 8*
Temperatures:		Temperatures:	
Max:	*Min:*	*Max:*	*Min:*

	December 7		*December 8*
Temperatures:		Temperatures:	
Max:	*Min:*	*Max*	*Min:*

December 9	*Additional Greenhouse Notes:*
Temperatures:	
Max: *Min:*	
December 9	
Temperatures:	
Max: *Min:*	
	When the container bulbs show leaf growth, move them to a brighter location.

December 10	*December 11*
Temperatures:	Temperatures:
Max: *Min:*	*Max:* *Min:*
December 10	*December 11*
Temperatures:	Temperatures:
Max: *Min:*	*Max* *Min:*

	December 12		December 13
Temperatures:		Temperatures:	
Max:	*Min:*	*Max:*	*Min:*

	December 12		December 13
Temperatures:		Temperatures:	
Max:	*Min:*	*Max:*	*Min:*

December 14	December 15
Temperatures:	Temperatures:
Max: *Min:*	*Max:* *Min:*

December 14	December 15
Temperatures:	Temperatures:
Max: *Min:*	*Max* *Min:*

	December 16	*Additional Greenhouse Notes:*
Temperatures:		
Max:	*Min:*	
	December 16	
Temperatures:		
Max:	*Min:*	
		Plan and order next years seeds from the new seed catalogs.

December 17	December 18
Temperatures:	Temperatures:
Max: *Min:*	*Max:* *Min:*

December 17	December 18
Temperatures:	Temperatures:
Max: *Min:*	*Max* *Min:*

December 19	*December 20*
Temperatures:	Temperatures:
Max: *Min:*	*Max:* *Min:*

December 19	*December 20*
Temperatures:	Temperatures:
Max: *Min:*	*Max:* *Min:*

December 21	*December 22*
Temperatures:	Temperatures:
Max: *Min:*	*Max:* *Min:*

December 21	*December 22*
Temperatures:	Temperatures:
Max: *Min:*	*Max* *Min:*

	December 23	Additional Greenhouse Notes:
Temperatures:		
Max:	Min:	
	December 23	
Temperatures:		
Max:	Min:	
		Repair any greenhouse draughts to save on heating costs.

December 24	*December 25*
Temperatures:	Temperatures:
Max: *Min:*	*Max:* *Min:*

December 24	*December 25*
Temperatures:	Temperatures:
Max: *Min:*	*Max* *Min:*

December 26	*December 27*
Temperatures:	Temperatures:
Max: *Min:*	*Max:* *Min:*

December 26	*December 27*
Temperatures:	Temperatures:
Max: *Min:*	*Max:* *Min:*

December 28	*December 29*
Temperatures:	Temperatures:
Max: *Min:*	*Max:* *Min:*

December 28	*December 29*
Temperatures:	Temperatures:
Max: *Min:*	*Max* *Min:*

December 30		*December 31*	
Temperatures:		Temperatures:	
Max:	*Min:*	*Max:*	*Min:*

December 30		*December 31*	
Temperatures:		Temperatures:	
Max:	*Min:*	*Max:*	*Min:*

Notes or Photos

A Note from the Author

As you browse through your daily record of greenhouse activities, you will notice all your accomplishments as well as the difficulties you encountered. With this comprehensive collection of reference data, you can now plan for the upcoming year.

The notes regarding seed propagation, transplanting and the fertilizing schedule will show whether these activity dates need to be adjusted in the upcoming year.

Daily temperature records indicate if adequate greenhouse ventilation and heating was maintained. For any additional greenhouse equipment, you will find several greenhouse and accessory companies listed in the final section of this journal.

The seed catalogues have just arrived, and it is time to plan and order for a new greenhouse season. Owning a greenhouse gives you the opportunity to try new plant varieties. You can find these listed under new plant introductions in the seed catalogues.

I know you have enjoyed gardening in your greenhouse over the past year, and I wish you continued enjoyment and success.

Greta Heinen

Greenhouse Gardening Tips

WINTER GREENHOUSE

Greenhouse heating requirements are always based on the minimum night temperatures.

Cool Greenhouse:	40°-45°F (5°-7°C)
Warm Greenhouse:	55°F (13°C)
Hot Greenhouse:	65°F (18°C)

Since very cold spells can occur from December to February, it is best to keep a close watch on the greenhouse night temperatures and set the heating thermostats accordingly.

Weather permitting, slightly open a vent during the day. Watch for cold draughts or a sudden drop in temperature in the greenhouse.

The continual movement of a small circulating fan will distribute the heat evenly. Constant air circulation can greatly reduce condensation.

Plants tend to stay drier during the winter greenhouse season. This is especially true in a cool greenhouse since the plants are not flowering but are in their dormant stage.

Winter is also a good time to plan for the upcoming season. Check the seed catalogues for greenhouse seeds, especially the tomato and cucumber varieties.

Start the varieties of slower growing plants in January and February.

SPRING GREENHOUSE

Spring is an exciting new season in the greenhouse for sowing seeds, transplanting and nurturing plants to maturity. It is also the time of year when the greenhouse environment needs more attention. Bright, sunny days and cool nights will cause temperature fluctuations.

Early in the spring season, the greenhouse still requires heating. A heated propagation area for seedlings and cuttings will save on heating costs.

An automatic vent opener can open the vents when the temperature rises in the greenhouse and close them as the outside temperature drops. The movement of a circulating fan will help equalize the greenhouse temperature.

If you have applied an interior liner to save on heating costs during the winter months, remove it during the spring season.

Direct sunlight can quickly overheat a greenhouse. Exterior shading is the most effective method of preventing heat build-up.

Increase watering and start a fertilizing schedule. It is recommended that these tasks be done in the morning.

Start bedding plants, tomatoes, cucumbers and peppers. A grow light fixture will add a few hours of additional light and give a boost to seedlings and cuttings.

The spring greenhouse is filled with seedlings and cuttings that are quickly maturing into plants. "Pinching back" these plants will encourage new branches. They will be moved outdoors, but a period of acclimatizing or "hardening off " needs to take place.

SUMMER GREENHOUSE

There is a noticeable change in the greenhouse after you have moved all the hanging baskets and bedding plants outdoors. Tomatoes and cucumbers have developed to the point that they now need more room.

Night heating is no longer required. During the summer months, the major task is to keep the temperatures down.

By keeping a record of the maximum temperatures during the day, you can determine whether more ventilation is required. Some options include exterior shading or an exhaust fan in warmer climates. Be sure that you open the roof vents, side vents and screened doors for cross-ventilation.

Give daily attention to watering the plants and crops in the summer greenhouse. On hot summer days, hose down the floor and benches. This "damping down" not only increases humidity but also brings down the temperature.

The greenhouse environment is humid and warm, ideal for pests and diseases. Check the plants daily as a preventative measure to ensure that no outbreaks occur.

Plants and crops are actively growing. By following a fertilizing schedule, you will ensure the best results.

In August, the garden is at its peak. This is the best time to take cuttings from geraniums, fuchsias and other varieties that you have decided will be part of next year's garden.

FALL GREENHOUSE

Fall is an unpredictable season. Sometimes it can be an extended summer; at other times it can be the start of an early winter. The fall days are shorter and the nights are noticeably cooler.

During the fall months, spend some time doing an annual cleaning and disinfecting of the greenhouse. Wash the inside and outside of the greenhouse, benches, shelving and plastic pots.

Remove shading material and install a plastic liner on the inside of the greenhouse. Insulating the greenhouse will certainly save on heating costs.

Check the greenhouse heaters and set the thermostat to low for any unexpected cold nights. Also, check the soil cables and prepare the heated propagation area for additional cuttings. Record the maximum and minimum temperatures in the greenhouse.

Continue opening vents on warm days to maintain an optimal environment for the plants. A circulating fan placed on a high shelf will move the warm air from the peak of the greenhouse to the plant level.

The tomato and cucumber season has now finished, and you can bring in the frost-sensitive plants for the winter. Check to ensure that all plants are pest-free before bringing them into the greenhouse.

The cuttings are ready for transplanting. Reduce the watering of the greenhouse plants. For the prevention of pests and diseases, inspect the plants frequently and remove all yellowing or dead leaves.

Suppliers of Greenhouse Kits and Accessories

B.C. Greenhouse Builders Ltd., A5-19327-94 Ave., Surrey, B.C., Canada V4N 4E6 1-888-391-4433
www.bcgreenhouses.com

ACF Greenhouses, 380 Greenhouse Drive, Buffalo Junction, VA. USA 24529 1-800-487-8502
www.littlegreenhouse.com

Advanced Solar, 701 N. Duncan Ave. Amite, LA , USA 70422, 985-748-5163
www.advancedgreenhouses.com

BackYard Greenhouses, 2549 Dougall Ave., Windsor, Ontario, Canada N8X 1T5 1-800-665-6263
www.backyardgreenhouses.com

Charley's Greenhouse Supplies, 17979 State Route 536, Mount Vernon, WA. USA 98273 1-800-322-4707
www.charleysgreenhouse.com

Clear Choice Glass Construction, 33389 Rainbow Ave, Abbotsford, B.C. Canada V2S 1E6 604-854-4388
www.ccgreenhouses.ca

Davis Contruction, 572 Peto Place, Victoria, B.C. Canada V8Z 2K6 250-727-0067

Everlast Greenhouses & Solarium Ltd., 13225 Trewhitt Road East, Oyama, B.C., Canada V4V 2B1 1-800-330-2919
www.everlastgreenhouses.com

Garden Retreat, 201-60th Ave, S.W. Calgary, Alberta, Canada T2H OB1 1-888-298-7097
www.buyagreenhouse.com

International Greenhouse Company, 1644 Georgetown Road, Danville, IL, USA 61832, 217-443-0600
www.igcusa.com

Seed Catalogues

Burpee Seeds, 380 Park Ave., Warminster, PA. USA 18991
1-800-888-1447
www.burpee.com

Dominion Seed House, P.O. Box 2500, Georgetown, Ontario, Canada
L7G 5L6 1-800-784-3037
www.dominion-seed-house.com

Harris Seeds, 355 Paul Road, P.O. Box 24966, Rochester, NY. USA
14624-0966 1-800-514-4441
www.harrisseeds.com

McKenzie Seeds, 30-9th Street, Brandon, Manitoba, Canada R7A 3E1
1-800-665-6340
www.mckenzieseeds.com

Park Seed Company, 1 Parkton Ave., Greenwood, SC. USA 29647-
0001 1 800 845 3360
www.parkseed.com

Stokes Seeds, P.O. Box 10, St. Catherines, Ontario, Canada L2R6R6
1-888-834-3334 USA 1-716-695-6980
www.stokeseeds.com

The Territorial Seed Company, P.O. Box 158, Cottage Grove,
Oregon,USA 97424-0061 1-888-657-3131
www.territorial-seed.com

Thompson & Morgan, P.O. Box 1308, Jackson, New Jersey, USA
08527-0308 1-800-274-7333
www.thompson-morgan.com

William Dam Seeds, Box 8400, Dundas, Ontario, Canada, L9H 6M1
1-905-628-6641
www.damseeds.com

Veseys Seeds, P.O. Box 9000, Charlottetown, PEI., Canada C1A 8K6
1-800-363-7333
www.verseys.com

Greenhouse Gardening Books

Gardening In A Cool Greenhouse
A Month-By-Month Beginner's Guide
Author: *Greta Heinen*
www. birchpublishing.com

Greenhouse Gardening Campanion
Author: *Shane Smith*
www.greenhousegarden.com

The Greenhouse Expert
Author: *D.G. Hessayon*

Gardening In Your Greenhouse
Author: *Mark Freeman*

All About Greenhouses
By *Ortho Books*
www.ortho.com

Greenhouses
Author: *Fiona Gilsenon*

Growing Successful Orchids
Author: *Mark Issac-Williams*

Greenhouse Gardening Websites

The Hobby Greenhouse Association
www.hobbygreenhouse.org

American Orchid Society
www.orchidweb.org

Cactus and Succulent Society
www.cssainc.org

International Geranium Society
www.intgeraniumsoc.com

Hydroponics
www.growingedge.com

B.C. Greenhouse Builders Order Form

Fax Orders: 1-604-882-8491. (Send this form)

Telephone Orders: 1-888-391-4433

Email Orders: inquiries@bcgreenhouses.com

Postal Orders: B.C. Greenhouse Builders Ltd
                           A5-19327-94 Ave
                           Surrey, B.C. Canada V4N 4E6

Name:_____

Address:_____

City:_____   Prov/State_____

Zip/Postal_____

My Greenhouse Journal
      $14.95 Cdn $10.95 US $_____
Mailing Charges
     $ 2.00 Cdn $ 4.00 US $_____

                     Total $_____

Payment VISA OR MASTERCARD Credit Card

Card Number:_____

Name on CARD:_____

Expiry Date: _____